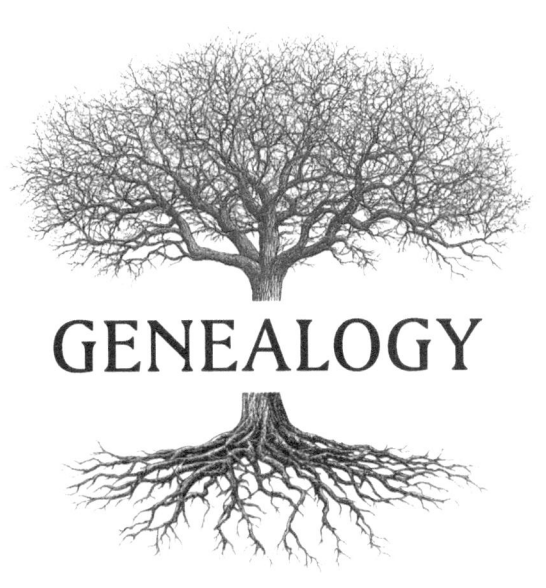

GENEALOGY

PAM O'BRIEN

DOS MADRES

2025

DOS MADRES PRESS INC.
P.O. Box 294, Loveland, Ohio 45140
www.dosmadres.com   editor@dosmadres.com

Dos Madres is dedicated to the belief that the small press is essential to the vitality of contemporary literature as a carrier of the new voice, as well as the older, sometimes forgotten voices of the past. And in an ever more virtual world, to the creation of fine books pleasing to the eye and hand.

Dos Madres is named in honor of Vera Murphy and Libbie Hughes, the "Dos Madres" whose contributions have made this press possible.

Dos Madres Press, Inc. is an Ohio Not For Profit Corporation and a 501 (c) (3) qualified public charity. Contributions are tax deductible.

Executive Editor: Robert J. Murphy

Illustration & Book Design: Elizabeth H. Murphy
www.illusionstudios.net

Typeset in Adobe Garamond Pro & Weibai SC
ISBN 978-1-962847-28-5
Library of Congress Control Number: 2025938696

For the First Friday poets.
Thank you for sharing your stories.

TABLE OF CONTENTS

INTERLUDE

THE OLDER YOUNGERS

THE YOUNGER YOUNGERS

SOLILOQUY

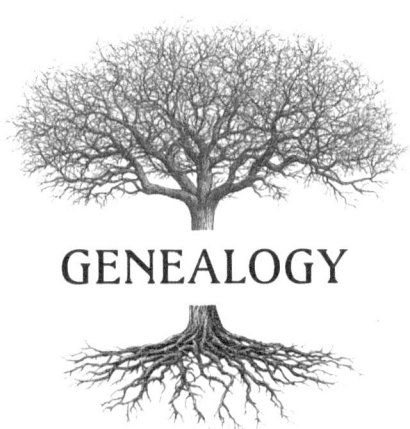

GENEALOGY

Who knows if this might be my last book. I'm 76.

There is a Jewish synagogue/museum in Prague
where a tape speaks the names of the Holocaust dead
over and over. Someone told me that Jews
needed to be able to trace their genealogy
back seven generations in order to speak in synagogue.
Jesus could trace his genealogy back 42 generations.

There is something to be said for saying the names,
telling the stories, remembering that to know who we are
we need to know who we were.

We all tread on the stories of our families.
They are the road.

Why I Garden

Memory lives in a place that looks
like my perennial garden.
She wears Turk's Cap lilies and shadows.
She plays in the waterfall, pitches
pebbles, watches drops fall through
her fingers. She understands we live in now,
this moment. Yet her name
is Memory.

I dig in dirt and she buzzes snapshots
my father grilling hot dogs
my grandmother knitting fisherman sweaters
my daughter painting a neon green plaster kitten
my husband mumbling in his sleep

my tears as I climb off a plane in Madrid
my tears as I hold my first grandchild
my tears watering all those gardens in all those places.

This is Memory's workplace.
My work is to notice.

THE ULTRA ELDERS

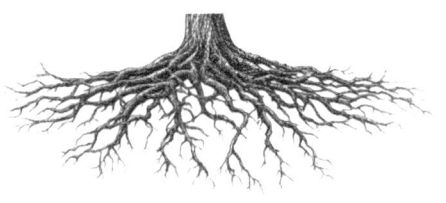

HALLELUJAH

My grandparents used the lace tablecloths, the good china
for every occasion they could think of.
They wanted family together,
eating, drinking, playing cards.
Once, after a bad flu season,
they held a hallelujah party
and even ordered a bakery cake.
The cake arrived with "Allayluya" in blue
on the white icing.
There were at least 30 of us laughing that night.
Then we played euchre.

Those grandparents grew up in World War I,
raised their families in the Great Depression,
lost their businesses, their jobs,
sold a lace tablecloth or two.
They gave their children to World War II.
They didn't have much or need much.
Homemade afghans covered the bare spots on couches.
They grew pole beans and dahlias in the back garden bed.
They read Readers Digest Condensed Books,
took Sunday drives, pieced together jigsaw puzzles,
planned lace tablecloth events.

I grew up with this.

And then watched my children
grow away from this,
move away, host only small casual parties.
Eventually I left too

for a retirement community in Florida
where I have everything I want
but not everyone I want.
Partly because I want my grandparents back.

I wonder if we might re-learn to throw
big parties just to be together again,
if we might dig out the good china,
the lace tablecloths.

Right Out In Front

Stan, my maternal grandfather, remembered for his magic tricks,
quarters appearing under our clean plates
or from behind my five-year-old ears,
or for his fancy Lincoln that he drove too fast
or his neon sign business, would take
the whole family to lunch or dinner at any restaurant
that boasted his newly installed sign.

How that man could eat.

As I grew older, he grew fatter,
then sicker. He tried to stay involved,
offered my mother $100 to quit smoking.
He was the one who wanted me
to go to college. He hugged me so close
when I got in, got a full scholarship,
offered me $100 if I majored in education.

The weight, the heart attack,
the first family death.
Then the missing of Stan.

I still see him strutting with the Shriners
band in every fourth of July parade.
I still remember how he sneaked
Nancy Drew mysteries and a flashlight into my room
when I had the German Measles
and had to recover in the dark for two weeks.

He probably ruined my eyesight
but he taught me to see.

NOTICE

Back then being noticed
came easy as breathing.

So easy I wasn't thinking
about developing what
would get me through
once I wasn't 16, 18, 20.
Thank God for the grandmother who nagged—

Your behind won't stay that size forever.
You need something to fall back on.
> *Learn to tend roses.*
> *Do needlepoint.*
> *Read the classics.*
> *Grow beef tomatoes.*
Even paint by numbers is a hobby.
I know, you could write.
You can't count forever on a man to notice you.
Some of the time girlfriends will get you through.
Most of the time you need to notice yourself.

LOSING NANA

When Nana announced she could no longer take
care of her apartment, cook lamb,
mend our clothes, bowl twice a week,
said she wanted to go to a nursing home,
the family was sad but acted quickly.
She was 84, surely a ripe old age,
and her broken ankle wasn't healing right.

We moved her into the Lutheran Home
the only one in town with an empty room,
divvied up the crystal, the quilts, the fancy soaps,
decorated her new room in the colors she wanted.

We thought she was going there to do
her usual in a new way—make friends,
check on her neighbors, play cards,
roll her hair into a French twist.
She may have thought that too,
the first month.

She soon realized she was not
going back to her apartment.
This new home was where she would die.
And it was a slow dying—years—
a long time to become bitter, lonely, lost.
At every visit, she cried, said
"I can't believe it has come to this."

I could still remember the Nana
I loved, hold that past into the present.

Not so with the great-grandchildren
who dreaded going to see her,
hated to hug her sloped shoulders,
hold her shaking hands

I plan to go swiftly before the slow leaving part.

As if I could control such a thing.
As if I could moisturize her feet
just one more Saturday morning.

Still So Many Days I Want Her Back

I want to see Nana fertilize her Jackson Perkins roses,
help her play solitaire while listening to the Cleveland
Indians on the radio.
I want her to tell me why my German potato salad doesn't
taste like hers.
I want her to hem my dresses and make my marble
birthday cake.

I want to hear her words again.

At my first wedding, she told me
there would only be room
for one shining star in the relationship
and it wouldn't be me.
I should have listened.

When she was 80,
she told me she liked it because
there wasn't as much peer pressure.

When I was in college, I told her
Aunt Sally seemed sad,
I whispered, "Nana, I think
something's happened to her."
She put her arm around me, whispered back,
"Honey, something happens to everyone."

GRAMPA CARL

Rosaly says an acceptable form
of Japanese psychotherapy
is to chronicle your gratitude debts.

I thought his gifts were
the paint-by-numbers kits,
the Nancy Drew books,
the week at his farmhouse in summer
when the Erie County Fair came to town
and we would walk the midway
munching on hot dogs and popcorn,
the aerograms arriving each Friday
the year I lived in Spain,
his movie camera recording every birthday,
wedding, Christmas, baptism.

And yet the greater debt

watching him
move his 85-year-old mother into his house,
take a job as a tool machinist after his business failed,
bury his daughter when she was 35,
introduce me always
as his beloved granddaughter.

At My Grandfather's Memorial Service

there in the social room of the
Salsbury Senior Living Apartments
in Erie, PA,
I greeted the old ladies
tottering in their black pumps
that matched large black handbags,
plumping white curls
that matched Sarah Coventry pearls.

I hugged them, smelled talcum and Estee Lauder.
I thanked them for coming.

"Oh, we loved to dance with Carl," every last one
of them, even the one in a wheelchair, said.
Dance? My 95-year-old, 5'4" grandfather dance?
Yes. Betty's time was 10am Tuesdays.
Myrtle would bring her own records
to Grampa's apartment Wednesdays at 1.

There was a set schedule, every day but Friday,
the day I came and cleaned his apartment,
took him to lunch and for a drive along the lake,
waited for him at the foot doctor,
waited at four different banks
while he checked his small savings account balances.

My grandmother who weighed
100 pounds more than Grampa, used a cane,
died an early death from dropsy,
never danced.

But Grampa,
(the ladies called him *sprightly* and *dashing*)
gave those gals what they missed most
the chance to be held
to be back at the cotillion.

GRACE

Grandma feared my father
would be her only child.
Grampa held her close at night
said *God will provide a new baby.*
They just needed to trust, to wait.
Grandma was bad at both.

One snowy Buffalo Saturday in 1931
she nudged Grampa awake
said *pack up Jackie, we're going*
to the orphanage on Maple Drive.
The old Ford stumbled its way across town.

Wandering the halls of the orphanage,
little Jackie whining because lunch was late,
Grandma grew confused.
I guess I was wrong she said.
Today's not the day.

Spring was stretching its way alive
when Grandma dragged Grampa
back for a second visit.
This time she knew right where to go,
which crib to head for,
which baby girl would nestle
into Grampa's chest
like it was the warm nest
she'd been hunting all week.
We're naming her Grace
Grandma told Grampa. *Hold her.*
This is what Grace feels like.

The Other One

Grandma pretended
her enormous size was no big deal.
Mornings after I'd slept over
she'd chuckle and invite little me
to watch as Grampa
laced her into her pink corset.
So many strings.
He even had to help her
slip her housedress over her head.
She said the arthritis hurt more
if she had to raise her arms.

Long after her death, Grampa told me
she was ashamed of being fat
tried all kinds of diets
cried herself to sleep sometimes.

Grampa was tiny and shiny and spry
had a full head of hair even into his 90s
would never have left the apartment
without some kind of hat
without his white shirt buttoned to the top
even at the 4th of July picnic.

After his stroke, we knew he didn't know
that they cut most of his hair off
that they lost one of his dentures.
that they called to tell us
he was standing naked in the
window of the nursing home.

Inside I hide the fat lady with
the precise little man,
and the other one who wants
to break out, to be exposed.

What We Keep

In my grandmother's kitchen I created art
well, paint-by-numbers pictures
once a horse, once an Indian chief.
Grandma talked non-stop as she lumbered
from fridge to stove to counter
an apron around her size 24 housedress.
I didn't listen very well
my painting consuming me
my legs dangling from the chipped blue chair
my arms stretching across the white table
to reach my paints.

I don't remember what Grandma was cooking
probably a pot roast
or what she told me
probably a story about
her trip to where Anne of Green Gables lived.
How we'd go there together some day.

But I still see those mornings
the tiny maple table lamp
lighting my painting
the sun through the window
making my grandmother shine.

THE YOUNGER ELDERS

Photo Of My Parents At 19

They look so young in this sepia photo
my father in his post WWII Army uniform
my mother slim back then
in a seersucker shirtwaist.
They stare pensively at the restaurant photographer
ignore their surroundings
glass salt and pepper shakers
half-eaten mounds of mashed potatoes
bread sticks in a tall glass.

I imagine them imagining
their November wedding
the apartment they'll paint
in my mother's favorite red,
the Chevy they'll save up for.
This for me, as their daughter,
is their photo of hope.

They know nothing yet
of unpaid bills, miscarriages, cancer.

They must have paid
the restaurant for this photograph.
It must have been a special night.

MUM

She was up by 6 am,
pink sponge rollers in her hair,
the smell of Pledge Furniture Polish rising like
her favorite perfume from the picnic table
we used in the kitchen.
She must have wanted a nicer table.
Or at least the money for one.
Coffee steaming in her chipped brown cup,
she was always full of caffeine.
Coffee, Coke, Tab if Coke wasn't on sale.
Eager for us to be off to school
so she could clean some more,
reminding us to do what the teacher said,
to do whatever we were told to do.

One fall, probably 1962,
while we were at school doing what the teacher said,
she walked to the dentist, had all 32 of her decayed teeth pulled,
walked home and lay crying on the couch when we returned.
Had I ever seen her cry before?
I don't remember.
She had trouble speaking but assured us
she would look better soon, not to worry.
She would get false teeth.

Could we not afford to have dental work done?
She cried more, then got up,
combed her tightly permed hair, made dinner,
vacuumed the living room
while she waited for my father to come home.

It was Fall. Soon we would be raking leaves
burning what I later realized
was nature's most beautiful display.
She would listen to the weather report
on her transistor radio, warn us of impending storms.

Soup

Much of what my mother did involved soup
September to May in Erie,
Erie typically full of rain or snow.
She stirred at the second-hand gas stove
two pounds beef stew meat
two packages mixed vegetables, the kind with okra
two cans stewed tomatoes
beef broth, lots of pepper
sometimes potatoes
sometimes noodles.
Simmer all day.

Coming home from school,
the smell would greet me even if she
barely glanced up from *One Life to Live.*
At 5:30 Daddy came home, always kissed her
said "something smells good."

Sometimes I write about my cold, distant mother
forgetting what Daddy knew
that all five of us would sit down in ten minutes
to her love language.
Hot crusty bread and that soup.

The Vermillion Villanelle

Red was my mother's favorite color.
When we asked, she always claimed red
but nothing about her was red.

Yes, she did own the red Christmas sweater
perched two poinsettias on the holiday hearth.
At Christmas, red was my mother's favorite color

but she filled our whole house with earth tones,
loved white gardenias the best.
Not much around her was red.

She hid anger, never flared up.
I never saw her dance or run.
Red—she said—was her favorite color.

In her crayon box, color didn't matter
if all were sharpened, better yet brand new.
Nothing about her screamed red.

When she was dying, she never
once cried. Never said goodbye.
Red was my mother's favorite color.
But nothing about her spilled red.

Today Is The 25th Anniversary
Of My Mother's Death

I thought I would be over her by now.
She didn't have to die, at least not then.
She could have agreed to dialysis, an operation.
But she didn't want to linger,
linger that's the word she used,
after Daddy died.
Nine years without him was plenty
she said.

She never did talk much
and she talked even less
that last week.
Once she asked me if she was dying
and I said *yes but*
you have options, treatments
that could turn that path around.
She dropped the subject
and asked if I would
dry shampoo her hair
and then style it.
So we did that.

She asked me to stay the night
in the hospital. That was the last night.
She stopped talking about 8 pm.

At 3 am the nurse nudged me
in the bedside chair, said
your mother is drawing

her last breaths. Drawing,
that's the word she used.
I crawled into her bed, hugged her,
told her all would be well
and that I would miss her.

How He Provided

My father smoked, back when smoking
was manly, sociable, didn't cause cancer.
Every day he was the first to rise,
made my fried egg breakfast,
packed two baloney sandwiches for his lunch
left 50 cents on the counter for my lunch
stuffed a new pack of Marlboro's in his shirt pocket.
I would hear his ancient Chevy backing out
of the driveway as the sun rose
as I pulled pink foam curlers from my hair.

I never thought of him as I walked
through my days of classes, cafeteria,
smiles from boys, notes from girls.
I never saw him at his drafting table
that perfect printing on the blueprints
those endless cups of coffee
that ashtray filling up.

He would walk in the door at 5:30.
I never saw him tired
but he must have been.
He never stopped at a bar
went out only to bowl or pick up groceries.

This is what he knew how to do.

ELEGY

My father was always owned by something—
first my grandparents
then the army
then, to make my mother happy,
the foundry credit union.

At the end
cancer consuming his lungs, his breath,
my father was owned by pain.

The last week
I would sit
next to his hospital bed
clutch my Styrofoam coffee cup
like it was the only heat
in an Alaska blizzard
call for more morphine
to hold off the pain
sing the songs he'd sung to me
and wanted to hear again
Ragtime Cowboy Joe
I'm a Lonely Little Petunia in an Onion Patch.

Yet
I imagine the pain
probably didn't seem
a stranger at all to my father.

Just another step.

THE WALK

I want to be as brave, as missed,
as my father.

My mother birthed me
when she was an unready 20
but my father
working too much,
too long, too hard,
he was ready
to read me *The Wizard of Oz* each night
to teach me to play cribbage
to drive his rusty green Chevy.

When he was 60
he grasped the hand of lung cancer
with both resignation and reluctance.
One day as I drove him to McDonald's
for a vanilla milkshake,
the only thing he could manage
after radiation, he said
"Even though this won't turn out all right
I have to walk through it."

A good walker, my father.
When he was gone,
I walked back to my busy husband
my sweet, voracious children
my piece of life in Erie
to dying slowly,
like each of us.

THE OUTER CIRCLE

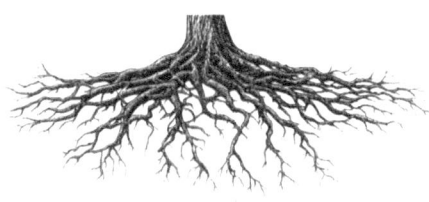

My Uncle's Memoir

I'm editing my uncle's memoir,
barely recognize my family story.
At 80, he wants to make amends
to my mother's dead sister, his wife,
because he thinks in some ways he killed her
and in some ways he's right.

Yes, his story confesses his alcoholism
but I can't find in his book
the night my aunt came to our door
with a black eye and three wailing children
or the day she threw his possessions
into the yard and set them on fire.

And nowhere in his text is
the story of his daughter, my cousin,
writing to me to write to my uncle to stop writing.
He keeps calling me and asking
for my memories. I don't want to remember.
I don't want to read his damn book. Ever.

DAVID MEANS "BELOVED"

They told Aunt Sally no regular school for him,
he would need a sheltered workshop.
Sally created her own workshop at home,
coached him in catching a ball,
taught him letters and numbers,
found risk-taking surgeons to operate on his twisted spine.
In spite of what they said.
In spite of her drunken husband.

And little David went off to school, regular school,
in a spinal brace. But school.
And then college.
He became a teacher for special needs kids.

Sally left for an urn in Laurel Hill Cemetery.
But not before she gave her boy
a map, a treasure chest.

Ode To Ireland As A Found Poem In Letters

The summer has been a disaster.
It has rained continuously.
                *

They are advising farmers with waste ground to sell,
we have about 9-10 acres waste hilly ground
and might give it a go.
                *

Any clothes will be very much appreciated
as clothes have gone a crazy piece here.
                *

The weather here is dreadful cold.
                *

Beef and milk are slashed in prices,
we can only hope for the best, it is terrible
to be working hard and getting poor
returns, everybody is saying this will be
a very poor little country by 1992.
                *

All the young people have left
the country looking for work.
                *

We have had the most dreadful summer here,
it never stopped raining.
                *

Between the weather and the large companies
folding up in this country
things aren't looking good.
And so many young people getting the cancer.
                *

We have had another bad year,

in fact worse than last year.
Lots of people didn't have crops
at all as some of the fields
proved too wet to work in.

*

This little country is very far away
from the markets in Europe,
it is being taken over
by foreigners, mostly Germans,
as the locals can't afford it,
and now hippies are moving in
and living on social welfare
so the middle class are the new poor.

*

The house inside had to be painted
as it got damp with all the rain
and any wallpaper just rolled down.

*

All the towns around here got flooded
and shops and their contents were destroyed.
Let's hope it is all behind us.

*

The health service is gone terrible.

*

But we kept consoling ourselves
that we were all in good health.

*

We are all well T.G.

*

I shouldn't complain when we have our health.

*

We are all fine T.G.

*

And yet, we had a lovely summer here,
lovely sunshine, the children were lovely.

(These letters were written by Margaret O'Brien, Ballwa,
Clonakilty, Ireland, to my mother-in-law Helen O'Brien,
Maggie Valley, North Carolina, 1980-1999. They
exchanged visits, letters and, on occasion, clothes for
children.)

TOO LATE

I climbed up the wall.
The wind answered me:
"Why so many little sighs
if it is already too late?"
Andalucian Siguiriya

Ed says "get me somewhere safe.
I need to be in a retirement place."
His daughters say that is his disease, his dementia, talking.
I call it the voice of reason.

Helen, hospitalized three times in six weeks,
refuses to move to assisted living.
"I won't live anywhere
that has more than one floor."

Lord, help these ancient in-law parents
entrenched in a lifestyle
they don't know how to leave
in spite of their children finding places for them,
offering to move them,

wanting to bring them close,
hold them tight,
push back their fears
of leaving their home,
fears not so much of leaving
as of dying.

We cannot buy them time.
It is already too late.

I WANTED TO BE RICH ENOUGH

to send John and Mary,
my younger brother and sister,
to college. College for me
came with great difficulty.
Family saw no value in it,
nor had the money to make it happen.

I was a first-generation scholarship girl
at Allegheny College, a ritzy liberal arts school,
earned book money, clothes money, cigarette money,
even the money for a Samsonite suitcase
to take my four skirts to college.
I worked two jobs on campus,
three those summers in Erie.
I counted coupons, waited tables, gave tours,
assisted in a lab, worked retail.

By the time
it was time
for John and Mary to think about college,
I was a mother, unhappily married
to a so-called playwright from a family
that gave him book money, clothes money,
three genuine leather suitcases.

John and Mary did just fine without me,
one a scholarship boy at Mercyhurst College.
the other a school secretary in Waterford.
And now I teach at a college.

But still, I wanted college
to be for them, a place
without any baggage,
without any price tag at all.

INTERLUDE

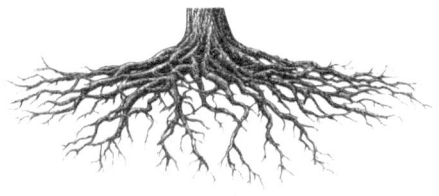

FAMILY TREE

Who I am
is my grandmother, my mother
and now my daughter.

We work too hard,
cook pot roasts and soups
whenever we can't be in control
of the world around us,
something that happens all the time.

We clean too much,
even closets and basement shelves.
We put up too many decorations
for every season, every holiday.

We forget to take care of ourselves.
We lie awake at night listening
for all that could go wrong.

We all love water
one tans on the Presque Isle beaches,
one reads by a pond,
one sails the Pacific Ocean,
one dives into the backyard pool,
in spite of the fear we all carry
of going too deep.

We are interchangeable,
those proverbial acorns falling,
falling too close.

And in each generation
I see us becoming
more like ourselves.

IN THIS SUMMER OF WET MEMORY

my houses are raining down on me,
all those places I've decorated and dug into,
polished and tuned.

The play houses I made as a child
with Nancy Drew books as floors,
tiny bricks and leftover wood from the garage,
where I created lives for
plastic Disney characters,
where I built my first artifacts, archives,
stories of adventure in the Wild West
or at the circus.

The upstairs flat on Market and North
where I learned to hang wallpaper
and make lasagna and leave my husband.

The too big, too much space
mother-in-law's house on 38th Street
where I never finished a to-do list
and taught myself how to drink
my way out of pain.

And now my English cottage
with a neighborhood free library
attached to the maple out front.

In this house one windy autumn night
magic found me and everything changed
so I don't believe I can live
without this house

and the garden has never been
more lush, more grand
than in this summer of rain.

Erie, PA

Now that I'm the age
when all my shoes hurt my feet
I miss the town on Lake Erie
miss being able to cross Forest Drive
go down 67 steps
and be on the rocky beach.

I miss the sand bars, seaweed,
huge waves in summer
packed brown leaves in fall
ice in winter
so thick you can walk out on it for a mile
and in spring the promise
of green that takes a long time coming.

I miss the flat streets, Ash, State, Chestnut,
the Italian restaurants, especially Martucci's,
the tiny wood 1950s-construction houses.

Mostly I miss the girl who lived there,
feel her behind my eyes in the mirror.
Some days, not often,
usually when my feet hurt,
I want her diving back into the lake
in her black bikini.

ANOTHER LOVE POEM TO YOU

This is not about skin
that largest organ of the body.
It's about breath
and what air we need to have
and how I need to breathe next to you.

There is no safety anymore
now that we are as old as
roller skate keys, glass milk bottles,
juke boxes. There is not much left us.

So I plan to stop thinking about time
forget the hustler winter moon
lurking just outside our patio door.
Instead let's fill up on
our tangle of stories
that catalogue our lives,
tell each other we will be all right,
practice that kind of magic
that alchemy of remembering.

GATHERING

Just when I think I've already lived
the happiest day of my life
along comes another surprise
from the universe

like last month when all three grown children
and their spouses and their children
came home for Christmas week.

They wanted to come.
They didn't fight.
Instead they played Clue
and went to church
and helped cook
and loved their ties and books
and carved wooden statues
we brought from Jerusalem.

The last night of all of us together
I watched the fireplace light washing
the walls. Even though it was winter
that room was again in full bloom.

I didn't think about losing
them back to their own busy lives.
I didn't mention that when
I look at them
I still see them
in their footed pjs.

The hustler winter moon
lurked right outside the window

but that night I was watching
the Chinese lanterns
glowing
flying
like silk on the nighttime deck.

THE OLDER YOUNGERS

HOME MOVIES

Joshua has taught himself Grampa's old trade.
He's bought a high-tech video camera
and now I watch as his baby, my granddaughter,
squirms in her high chair
toddles in a pumpkin field
yanks her barrette out
and throws it at the dog.
How I love being part of her life from a distance.

But there are still times
I need Grampa's old 8 millimeters,
now carefully preserved on DVD.
Those are the people I want back
and there we all are
in our nappies, lace aprons, best ties
in our confirmation suits and Easter dresses
tossing tinsel on the tree
carving the turkey
lighting the candles
flipping hamburgers on the grill
posing at every welcome to
you-name-the-state sign
carting our folding lawn chairs
to the 4th of July parade.

On iced winter nights
I crave hot chocolate
and family history
beating its way through my veins.

David Is Back On DVD

I thought I left David behind me forever
when we divorced. Goodbye.
Good riddance. All that.

Oh sure, we pass each other at graduations, weddings.
Once David called to ask me to help his mother.
He lived 3,000 miles away.
I was five minutes from her.
I smuggled cigarettes into her
assisted living village, drove her
to the hospital to visit her husband
dying from smoking.

But it's not over. David is back
because of the granddaughter we share.
David is back on the DVDs
our son sends. David rocks Maggie.
David sits at the Thanksgiving table
in the chair I'll be in for Christmas.
Maggie chases his dog around the living room.
His wife mashes the potatoes.

David is wealthy now, has a dog,
a wife who stays.
I hate it that we are still family
even as I realize that it's not just him
but my aversion to the woman I was.

Yet how I love our son,
our son we created,
our son who edits, splices,
writes new scripts to create
this video scrapbook family.

Linked In Ways He Doesn't See

The nine months I cradled
him under my heart,
the nights I slept
on the floor by his crib
sure if I left
he would smother,
that feeling
that his world
was shaky, tipsy
and the world out there
beyond his world
would tear him apart.

And then the coming apart.
This boy man who last night
told me he is moving in with Jeff,
not returning to college.
He will create art,
sell it, make a fortune.
He refuses to see the dentist.
Pieces of teeth are falling off.

I think *brilliant, lazy, artistic.*
Angry. Mostly a*ngry.*
The anger links us.

NOW THAT MY SON HAS A SON BUT NO WIFE, I WANT TO TELL HIM THIS

I am so proud that you
kept on after she left you
kept on for your son, that's what you told me
pushed through the loss, your own poor health
to a sadder, smaller place to call home
with your son there three days each week.

You've learned how the wounds grief sends
heal and then reopen. And you kept on
even when your job disappeared
in the pandemic.

I want you to tell your boy every day
that you love him. I'm not sure I did that enough
and trust me he won't believe it.
He will be scared in this new life sometimes
well maybe most of the time
and it will be easy for him to forget you love him.

But you just keep on saying you love him.
Some days he will say he hates you,
or at least hates what you're doing,
grounding him, making him do chores.

He doesn't really. Just keep on.
Draw a new map to where you live.
You will be all right.
Perhaps even more than that.

DAUGHTER

I wish my mother had told me
being her daughter wasn't going
to go all that well.
She was going to matter way too much
and I was going to end up
carrying her long past the heart attack,
the refusal of dialysis.

Even past the funeral
I'd be carrying her
into all those places she avoided
like the proverbial plague—
airports, libraries, oceans.
I expect I will never
leave her behind.

She is in my vegetable soup recipe,
the way I fold clothes.
Her dark hooded eyes stare
from the wedding picture in the guest room,
sultry, beautiful,
not smiling, not even then.

She called her mother every morning
at 9 am. I should have called her more.

I envision my own daughter
in her grown up LA life
sitting in the soft afternoon
sipping wine amid bougainvillea

in a garden café. She smiles
and confides to her friend,
"You know, I love her so much
but in some ways she's ruined my life."

MOTHERING

Molly is my dangerous child
the one who wandered away at amusement parks
took up risky competitions like high diving
and now the Transpac sailing race,
alone from San Francisco to Honolulu.

I imagined I wore my mother costume well with her
in spite of how it changed my college-girl body,
those leaking breasts, those puffy thighs,
that hip that never worked well again
after she bounced on it for two years,
and all that blood that came slipping
into the world she slid into.

Perhaps I never quite grasped losing
the woman I thought I would be
in exchange for being her mom.

Yet when she calls,
I still go running
on these tottering old limbs,
asking in a faltering voice
what can I do?
what do you need?
hoping that what she still needs is me
in spite of all I did to set her free.

Did my mother feel this same way
and I just didn't see it?
Did she understand

that along with the children comes
the sure knowledge that we secretly plan
to keep them, grip them, consume them,
that no matter who they are, like wolves,
we will raise them as our own.

Big Holidays

We did the holidays big.
Grandparents, aunts, uncles, cousins
jammed into one candle-rich dining room
passing gravy boats and olive trays
speculating on whether the cows
on Uncle Donny's farm would make it through the blizzard
whether Uncle Jerry would leave that damned Rockette
and come back to Aunt Grace.

Usually around coffee and pie time
Stan would move us all to remember
when he first saw Nana at the club in Schenectedy
when he bought the neon sign business
even though Nana said he'd lose his shirt
and now he drives a Lincoln.

I was six, eight, ten then.
Stan hadn't had his first, second, third heart attack.

I remember my mother, dark circles under her eyes
running from kitchen to table
smiling at Stan's jokes
refilling Uncle Herbie's highball glass,
my Shirley Temple.
Keeping us all going.

I put in my years of doing holidays big.
Silver, china, hors d'oeuvres, starched napkins
then collapsing the next day.
That's how we did it.

This year my newlywed daughter hosted her first holiday dinner.
Only six of us. Turkey in a deep fryer,
everyday dishes, Mickey Mouse flatware.
But we sat around that table for hours laughing
then headed off to the living room to play Trivial Pursuit.

WHAT IS UP

with these parents
who are also my children?
This isn't what I taught them.
This isn't what I wanted them to do.

Their children are the center of their lives
cars when the kids turn 16
trips to Paris and Hawaii
weekends devoted solely to kids' sports
summers packed with day camps
sleep away camps
helping the rest of the world camps
in Morocco and Costa Rica.

And these children
who are my grandchildren
never send a thank you
never do a chore.

And my one child
who has no children
wants me to pretend
I'm her dog's grandmother
and send pooch gifts.

And yet

I remember my grandparents
in their suits and ties
floral print dresses

whispering over their whiskey sours
that my parents were spoiling me,
creating a child who would never
be able to function
when the hard knocks of life hit.
As surely they would.

THE YOUNGER YOUNGERS

MAGGIE

> "Take heed…lest you forget the things
> your eyes have seen."
>
> Deuteronomy 4:9

I have my eye on Maggie
as the next storytelling steward for our family.
She's only 11
writes poetry
acts out stories with plastic horses
knits scarves for needy children at Christmas.

The others live beyond the stories,
live in future to-do list time.
They are busy making money, watching TV,
buying technology.
Or they are trying to cope with
skin diseases, eye problems, downsizing.

While I would still like to fix them,
I retreat a little each year
from the nurturer
to the recorder, the archivist.

And I watch.

I'm watching Maggie
to see if she will take up
the language of remembering

wear it
let it wear on her.

How To Heal Yourself

Maggie, we are living in hard times.
Being a teenager, being scared,
being alone makes being hard.
You are the artist granddaughter.
and art is blessing and curse for sure.

I offer you this.

Find what it is that will feed your soul
     a book about Gothic architecture
     a walk to the reservoir
     a picnic in your backyard with the dog
     a small dinner of tomato soup, grilled cheese.

Understand that this won't be
your only time of despair.
Life is up and then down,
rarely balanced for long.

Do things to take your mind off loneliness.
Do what you can to help someone else
so the next time dark descends
when you lose someone you love
or get sick
or can't find the path
you will be more ready.

Learn how to stop, to rest.
Most of us spend a lifetime
figuring that one out.

And as you go on,
because I know you will go on,
keep writing, keep painting,
keep going back over all of it.

Each time it will be new again.

GAVIN

the easy grandchild,
the happy one,
the laid back boy,

unless we saw you
solving puzzles in an Escape Room
       breaking codes, getting us out of chains,
       opening locked doors,
or if we noticed you
tracking, memorizing football scores,
       every team's standings for every Sunday afternoon,
or if we watched you
       with that red-haired Irish girlfriend
       full-on eye contact,
       your hand on her elbow,
       that strong softness no 16-year-old boy
       should possess.

You will make the way look simple.
Every space you live in, Gavin,
will be a house of deep greens
and hot cider on cold nights.
You will continue to startle us
       with how well you fit into this world.

ALEXANDER'S EYES

Since my tiny grandson
does not see
as I do, will he

know violets by their satin petals
their dust on his fingers

know carrots
not by orange
but by snap and crunch

know the ambulance
by its siren
then remember
to pray for those inside

know dancers at the wedding
by whirling in their midst
feeling the beat
feeling hands holding his
feeling hips swaying next to him.

Will he touch the stack of blocks
growing and say "Gramma,
I made a tower"?

And then will he say
"Come see."

MAPPING

My little grandson Alex loves maps,
the road maps from Triple A that
fold out and cover his car seat
or practically any atlas will do.
He loves to find
the Smoky Mountains and Lake George
places we've taken him.
He loves globes too.
He can find Nepal every time.
And of course Pittsburgh where he lives.

Alex lives in two places,
Mommy's house and Daddy's house.
I never hear him say "my house."
He prefers the maps—

ways to locate
where he's been
where he wants to go
maybe ways to avoid where he is
until he can figure it out.
In some ways, I think
he's creating a map
to where he wants to live.
He never speaks of this.
He's only six. How could he?

Already he understands
there is no safe place.

SOLILOQUY

BECKY TOLD ME

it's time for me to be done
cleaning, washing clothes,
making meals and dusting treasures.
It's time for me to be done with routine,
with following the rules.

Becky said it's fine to follow some rules
like be kind to other people
but those really aren't rules,
they are just our response to grace.

She told me to think
about my best day
that party in that house
with all the family there,
that light from that candle,
the truth of that day,
the comfort in that story.

Don't hold that day too tight though,
she said, don't squeeze it.
Hold it in open hands
let the sun shine on it
the breeze blow over it
and even if rain falls on your best day
it will only make it cleaner, clearer.

She told me there is only one thing.
It is always, always love.

The Best Day

was driving Alex from my daughter-in-law's house
to spend the day with me, to stay overnight,

reading highway signs,
I-79, turnpike, speed limit 65.

First stop at the German bakery,
then home for pancakes
always pancakes for breakfast.

At least two hours at the library
and so many books to bring home
we needed the large Ikea bag.

Trucks and boats in my garden by the waterfall,
Smiths hot dogs for lunch.

Afternoons we rode the light rail into the city
Potomac, Station Square, Steel Plaza
and turned right around to ride back home
always thanking the driver.

Watching a Peanuts movie
usually the one where Charlie Brown
traveled to France, more books.
Extra cheese pizza for dinner, always pizza.
His bubble bath with sea creature toys.

Then three stories, one fairy tale, one science,
one he picked from his library books.
He always knelt and prayed the same prayer
thank you God for everything and everyone
I like and love.

That day, over and over,
bent me, changed me, broke me,
put me back together.

Even though I had done these things
with my own children,
Alex, son of my son,
molded me into someone else
because of how he saw things
because of how he learned
because of how he liked and loved.

THE PLAN

"Tell me what it is you plan to do
with your one wild and precious life."
Mary Oliver

In this stage closer to death than birth,
I pace in a primitive hunger
to hunt, not relationships, but memories
to gather, not possessions, but words.

I remember
the house sparkling, the roast in the oven,
the children shaking snow from their coats,
the candles lit.
On my last day
I want to feast on that day.

I want to be completely used up when I go.
I want to have done more than I thought I could
    laughed more
    cried more
    ached more
    relished more
    worked harder
    played harder.

I don't want a tender, sweet body at the end.
I want to creak and groan and remember
    every bike ride
    every hike
    every bouncing horse
    every roller coaster

every baby whooshing from my body
every grandchild snugging on my lap

every single night of sweet, hot love.

Most of all, I want to have said
what I came here to say
that this dear life was worth it
that my faith tells me this is not the end
that my God has been and will always be there.

I want to have no words left.

ABOUT THE AUTHOR

 PAM O'BRIEN began writing poetry at Allegheny College with a response to the Beatles' song "Strawberry Fields Forever," something we probably shouldn't try to respond to. A former resident of Buffalo, Erie and Pittsburgh, she worked in the fields of writing grants, teaching Spanish and English and finally teaching Professional Writing at the University of Pittsburgh for nineteen years. Six years ago, she retired as a Professor Emerita to Florida.

In her new, warmer home, she volunteers at a local library and the VA, loves yoga and water aerobics and continues to write.

She has four chapbooks and a full-length poetry collection and has been frequently published in poetry magazines and journals. During Covid, she wrote a novella and hopes to publish it someday. Part of her Florida experience has involved starting a women's poetry workshop. That group is currently planning to publish an anthology of their stories.

She has three children (Boston, Pittsburgh and LA), three grandchildren and a mighty fine husband who also writes.

ACKNOWLEDGMENTS

Three of the poems in this collection appeared previously in the same or similar form.

"The Vermillion Villanelle", *Iodine Poetry Journal*
"Much of What My Mother Did", *Blue Collar Review*
"How We Hold On To What We Can't Keep", *Always Looking*

Of course, none of us can ever say, "I wrote this all by myself and no one helped me." Thank you to the Salisbury Hill Poetry Workshop (Chautauqua, NY), Berwyn Moore's graduate school poetry course (Erie, PA), the Squirrel Hill Poetry Workshop (Pittsburgh, PA) and the First Friday Poets (The Villages, FL).

Other books by Pam O'Brien
published by Dos Madres Press

The Answer to Each is the Same (2012)

For the full Dos Madres Press catalog:
www.dosmadres.com